Bot Maker

BUILD YOUR OWN INCHWORM BOT

Tucker Besel

BLACK RABBIT BOOKS

Hi Jinx is published by Black Rabbit Books
P.O. Box 227, Mankato, Minnesota, 56002.
www.blackrabbitbooks.com

Jennifer Besel, editor; Michael Sellner, designer;
Omay Ayres, photo researcher

Library of Congress Cataloging-in-Publication Data
Names: Besel, Tucker, author.
Title: Build your own inchworm bot / by Tucker Besel.
Description: Mankato, Minnesota : Black Rabbit Books, [2018] | Series: Hi jinx. Bot maker | Audience: Age 9-12. | Audience: Grade 4 to 6. | Includes bibliographical references and index.
Identifiers: LCCN 2017009965 (print) | LCCN 2017037521 (ebook) | ISBN 9781680723564 (e-book) ISBN 9781680723267 (library binding) | ISBN 9781680726503 (paperback)
Subjects: LCSH: Mobile robots—Design and construction—Juvenile literature. | Geometridae—Larvae—Models—Juvenile literature. Classification: LCC TJ211.415 (ebook) | LCC TJ211.415 .B473 2018 (print) | DDC 629.8/932—dc23
LC record available at https://lccn.loc.gov/2017009965

Printed in the United States.

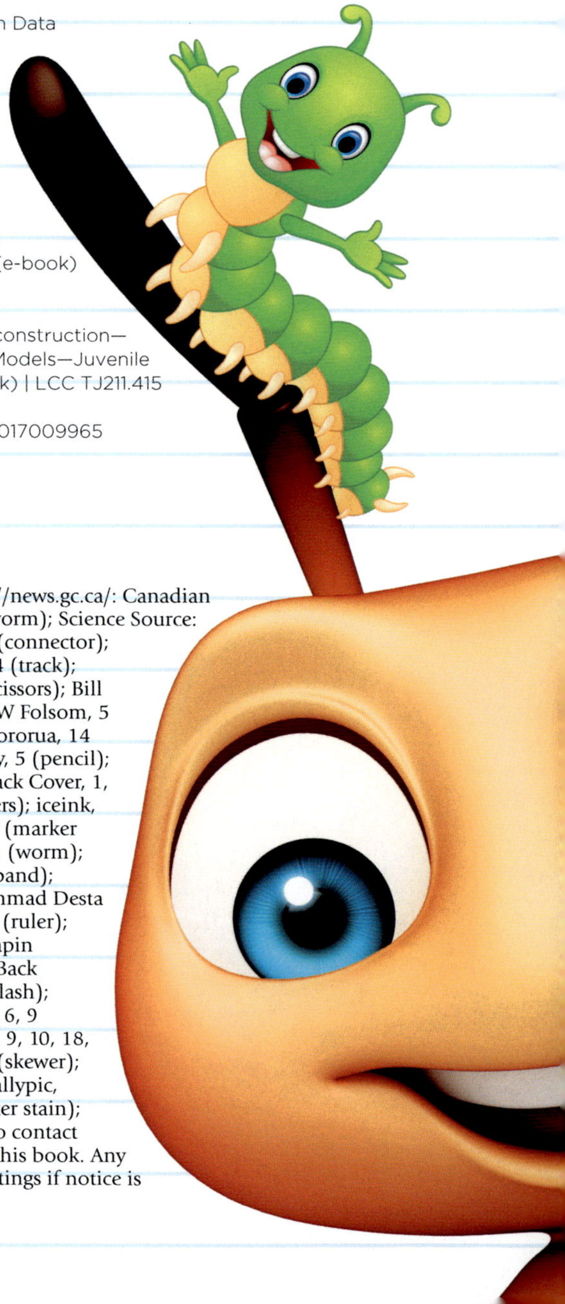

Image Credits

Grant Gould, all robot illustrations
Dreamstime: Simm49, 5 (alligator clip); http://news.gc.ca/: Canadian Armed Forces, 20 (l); iStock: Dualororua, 2 (worm); Science Source: NASA, 20 (r); Shutterstock: 7th Son Studio, 5 (connector); advent, 19 (kid); AlexLMX, 5 (battery); arbit, 4 (track); Art'nLera, 3, 12, 16, 21 (bkdg); belka_35, 5 (scissors); Bill Fehr, 5, 8 (screwdriver); Bplanet, 5 (motor); BW Folsom, 5 (straws); Carolyn Franks, 5 (cardboard); Dualororua, 14 (grasshopper); elbud, 5 (cap); Fedorov Oleksiy, 5 (pencil); Fleur_de_papier, 8 (tape); Galyna G, Cover, Back Cover, 1, 5, 7, 8, 11, 15, 19 (bkgd); hoomoo, 5, 12 (pliers); iceink, 5, 6, 7, 11 (glue gun); Ilya Chalyuk, 3, 4, 6, 20 (marker strokes); Jumnong, 5 (tape); Ken Benner, 7, 21 (worm); Marek Walica, 5 (wire); mayakova, 5 (rubber band); Memo Angeles, Cover, 19, 22 (worm); Muhammad Desta Laksana, Cover (tarantula); Nosopyrik, 5, 6, 7 (ruler); opicobello, Cover, 1, 12, 18 (highlighter); Orapin Thepsuttinun, 5 (cardboard); Pasko Maksim, Back Cover, 7, 10, 23, 24 (torn paper); PILart, 7 (splash); Pitju, 3, 16, 21 (curled paper); Pixel Embargo, 6, 9 (pencil); Rohit Dhanaji Shinde, Cover, 2–3, 6, 9, 10, 18, 22, 24 (ant); S K Chavan, 8 (cone); SeDmi, 5 (skewer); Teguh Mujiono, 9 (ladybug), 17 (cricket); totallypic, 7, 10, 12-14, 16, 17 (arrows); Tueris, 11 (marker stain); your, 18 (cloud) Every effort has been made to contact copyright holders for material reproduced in this book. Any omissions will be rectified in subsequent printings if notice is given to the publisher.

CONTENTS

Chapter 1
BE A BOT MAKER

Robots aren't just for TV. People make robots that walk, run, and fight. Even beginners can create bots that wiggle.

This book will help you create a simple inchworm robot. Robot building takes patience. Don't give up if something doesn't work. Experiment until it does. And, most importantly, have fun!

WHAT YOU'LL NEED

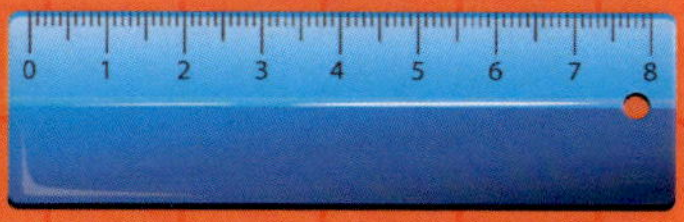

ruler

sharpened pencil

3 straws

4 identical soft drink bottle caps

1 2 x 6-inch (5 x 15-cm) rectangle of corrugated cardboard

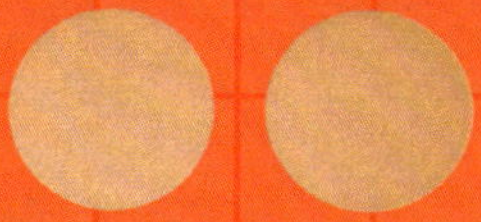

2 ¾-inch- (2-cm-) diameter circles of corrugated cardboard

2 1-inch- (2.5-cm-) diameter circles of corrugated cardboard

scissors

1 wooden skewer

1¼-inch (3-cm) alligator clip

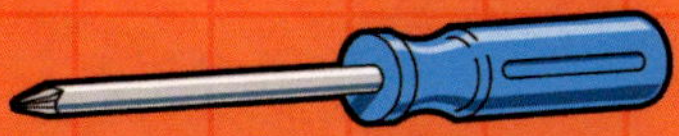

Phillips screwdriver

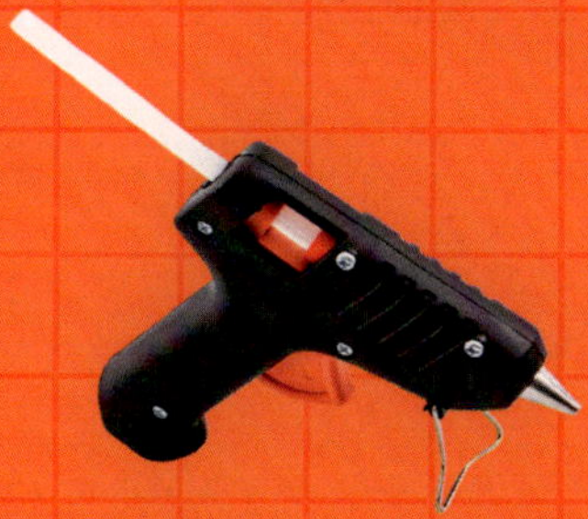

hot glue gun and hot glue

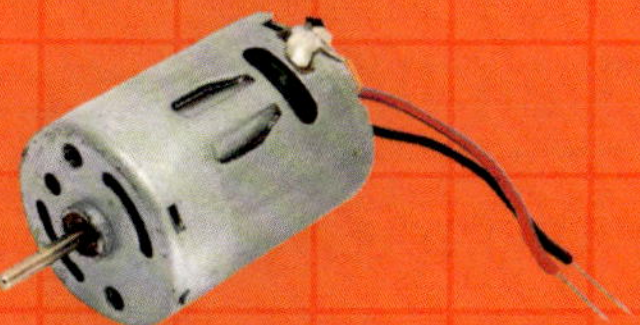

6-volt toy motor with wires (with ½ inch [1 cm] of wire exposed)

electrical tape

1 medium-sized rubber band

pliers

9-volt battery

9-volt battery snap connector (with ½ inch [1 cm] of wire exposed)

10 inches (25 cm) uninsulated 14-guage copper wire

Chapter 2

LET'S BUILD!

1. Cut each straw to a length of 2 inches (5 cm).

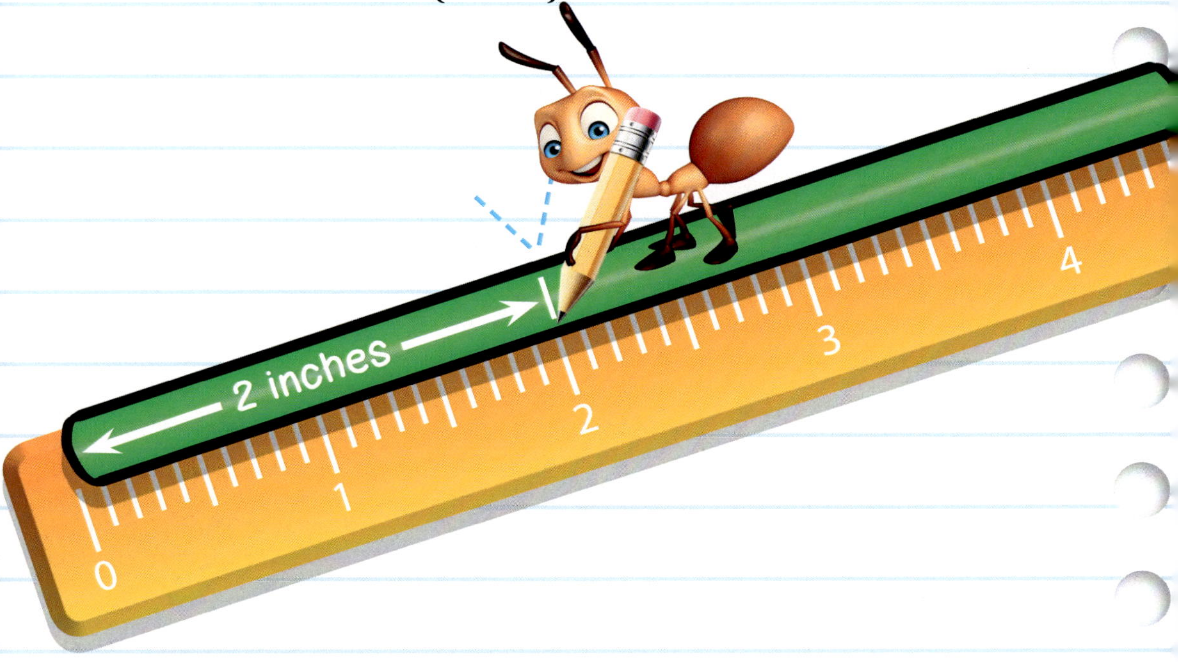

2. Bend the cardboard rectangle in half. Then lay it flat on your workspace.

3. Hot glue one straw ¾ inch (2 cm) from a short end of the rectangle. Repeat with a straw on the other end. Glue the third straw 1 inch (3 cm) from the bend. The half with two straws is the back of your bot.

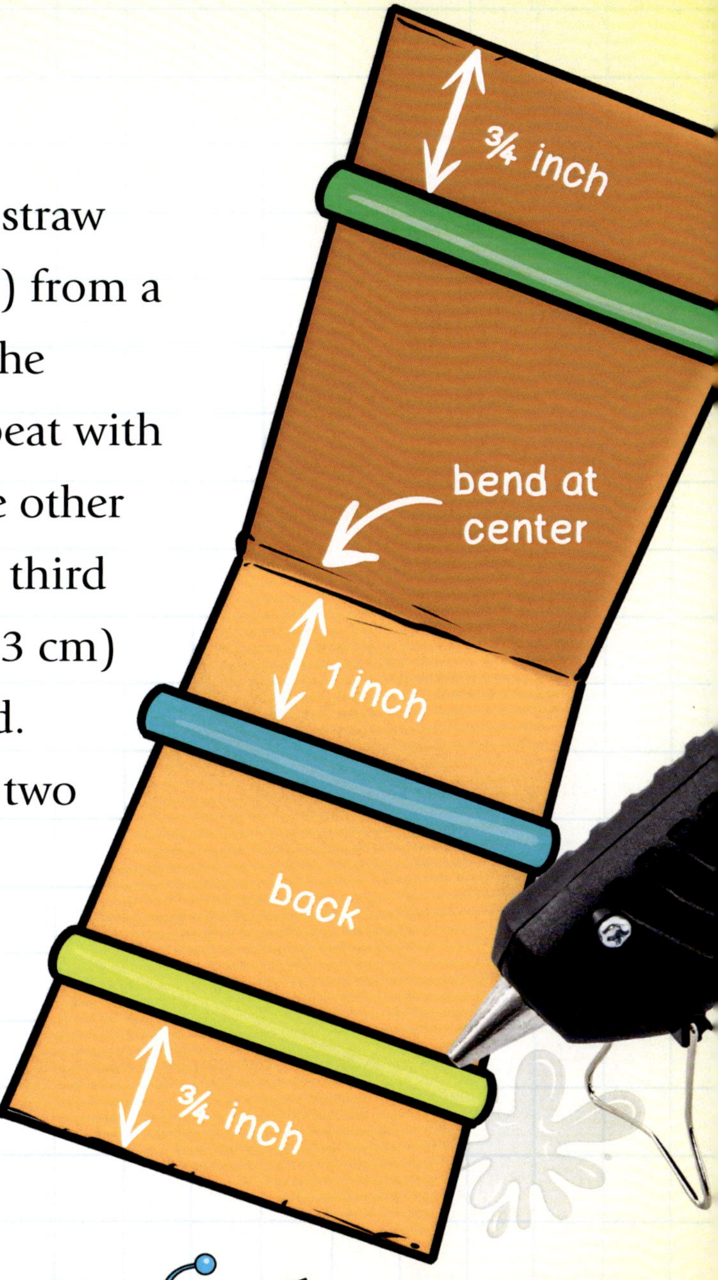

JOKE BREAK

Why was the inchworm mad?
It had to use the metric system!

4. Use the screwdriver to poke a hole in the center of each bottle cap.

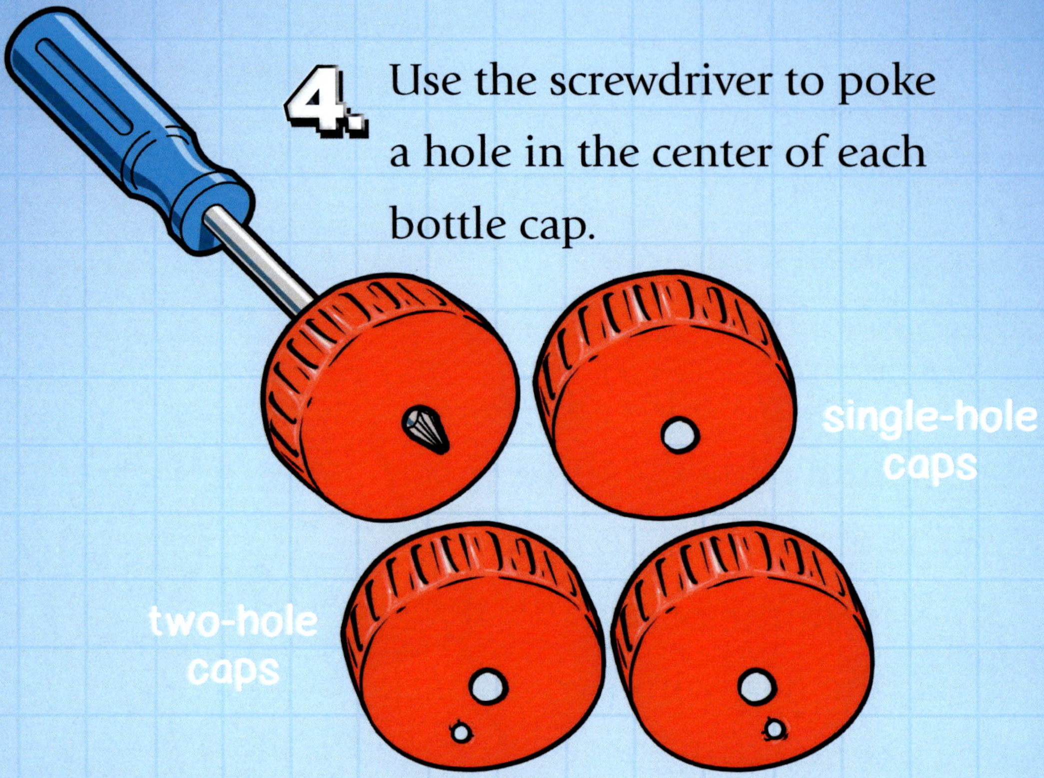

5. Poke a second hole in two of the caps. The holes should be near the edges of the caps. Make sure the holes are in the same places.

Have an adult help you poke the holes.

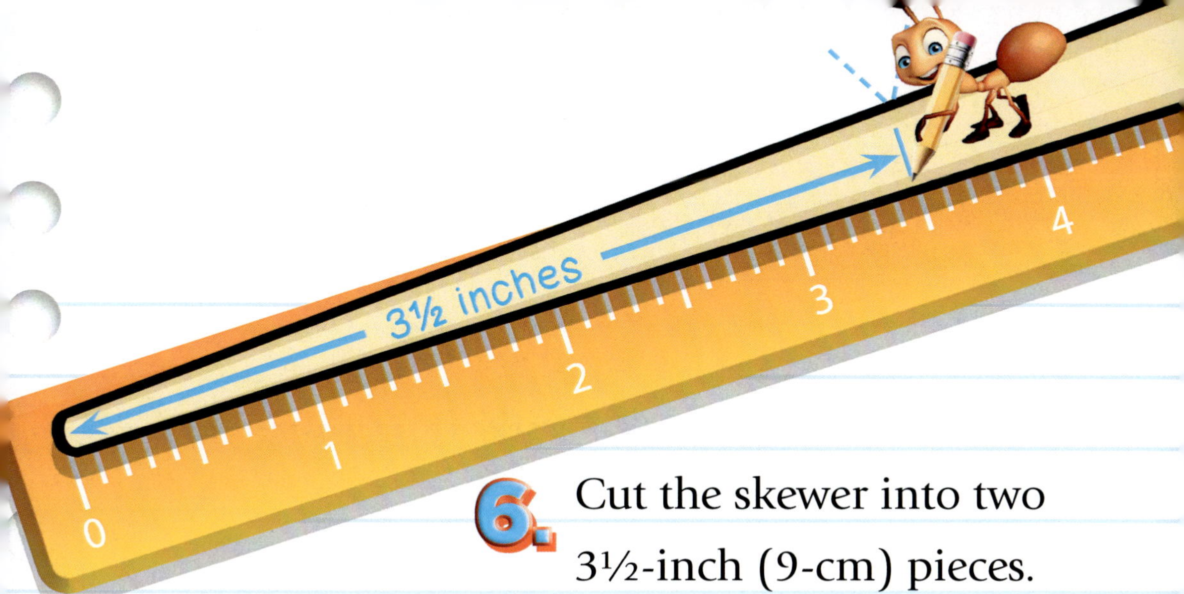

6. Cut the skewer into two 3½-inch (9-cm) pieces.

7. Slide a single-hole cap onto the end of one skewer piece. Face the top of the cap out. Hot glue it in place. Slide the skewer through the back straw on the cardboard. Then hot glue the other single-hole cap on.

Real inchworms have legs.
Yours is going to have wheels!

8. Slide a two-hole bottle cap onto another skewer piece. Hot glue the cap in place.

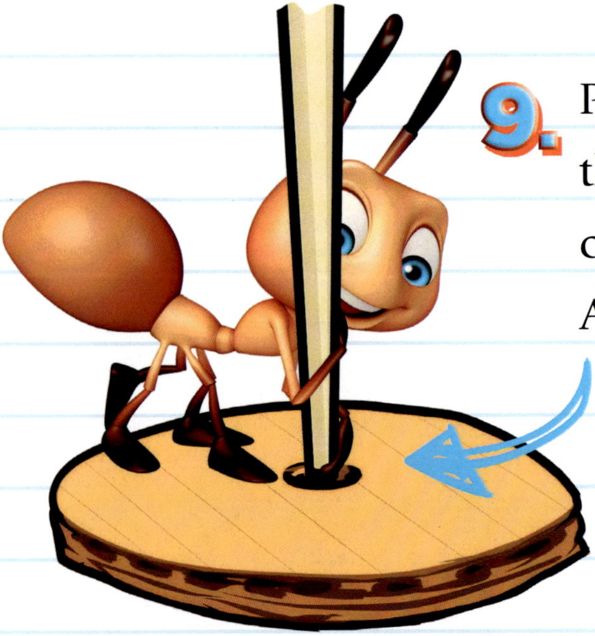

9. Poke a hole through the center of each cardboard circle. A skewer works well.

10. Sandwich one small circle between the two larger circles. Line up the holes. Hot glue them together.

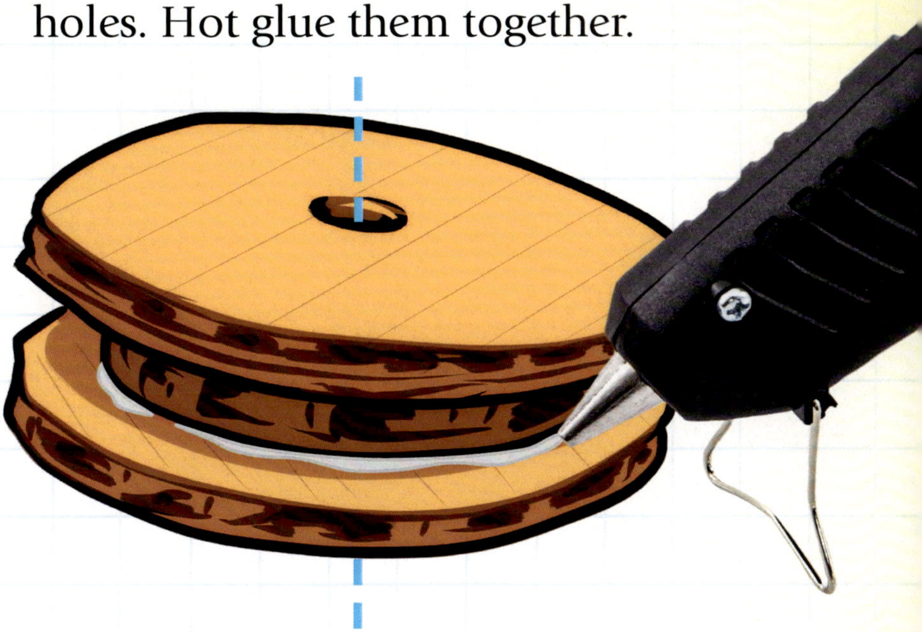

11. Slide the circle sandwich onto the skewer with the two-hole cap. Put the circles close to, but not inside, the cap. Hot glue the circles in place.

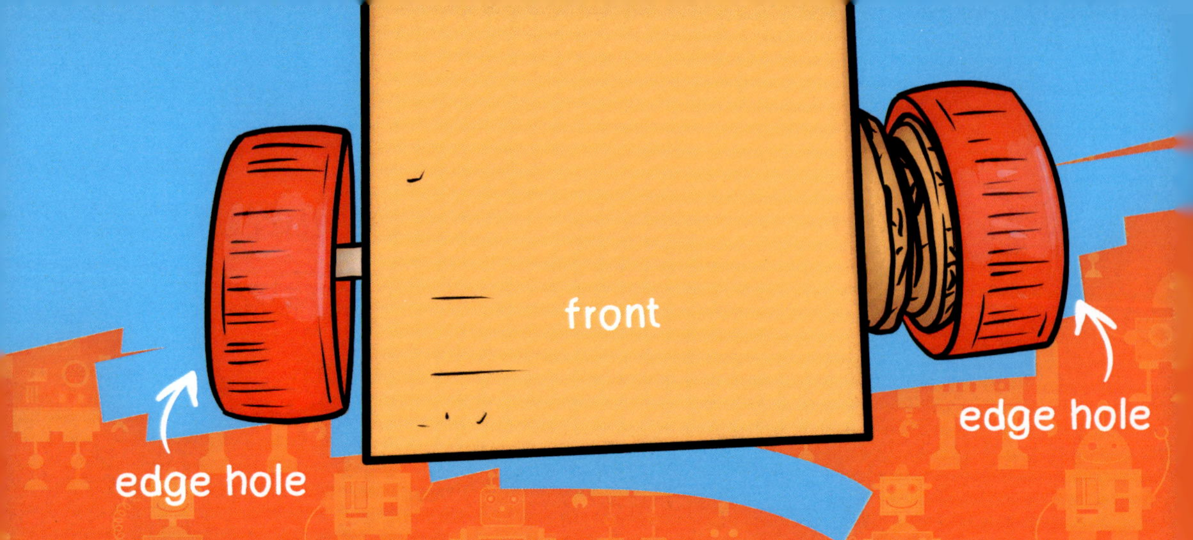

12. Slide the skewer through the front straw on the cardboard body. Put the last bottle cap on the skewer. Make sure the edge holes line up between the two caps. Glue the caps in place.

13. Attach the alligator clip to the red wire from the motor. To do this, put the wire between the tabs on the back of the clip. Then use pliers to pinch the tabs together.

14. Connect the black wires from the battery connector and the motor. Hold the exposed parts of the black wires side by side. Then twist the exposed ends together. Snap a battery into the connector. **Clamp** the alligator clip to the connector's exposed red wire. The motor's **shaft** should spin. Unclamp the clip.

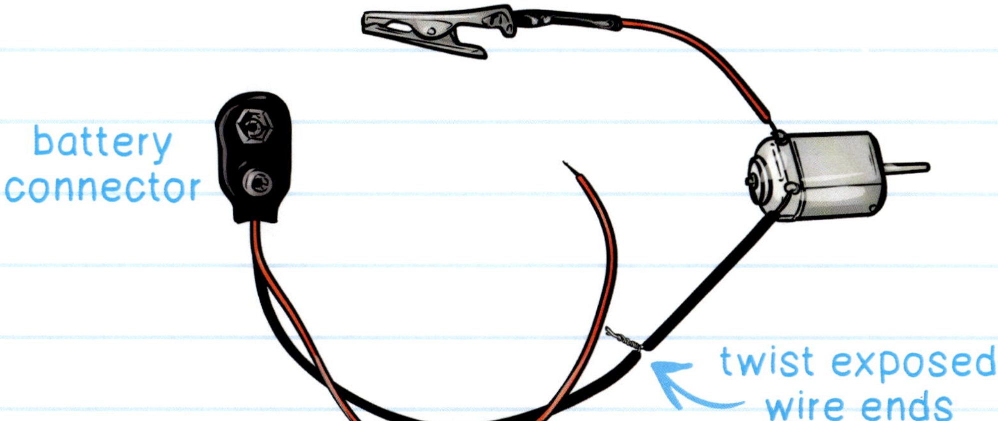

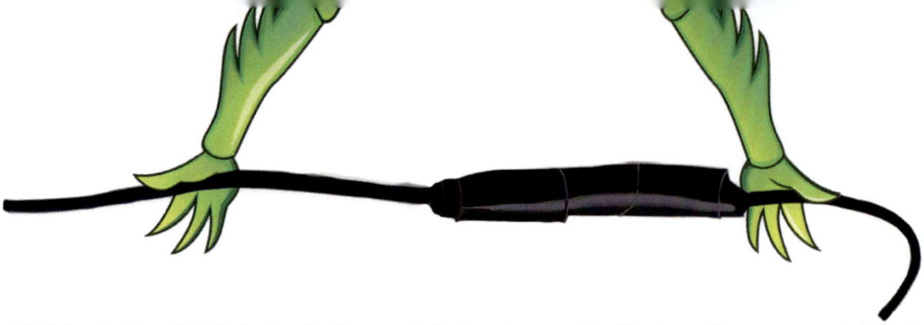

15. Bend the twisted wire ends down. Wrap them to the black wire with electrical tape.

16. Hot glue the battery to the back end of the cardboard. Point the wires toward the bend. Then glue the motor in front of the battery. Hang the shaft over the side. Line up the shaft with the cardboard circles.

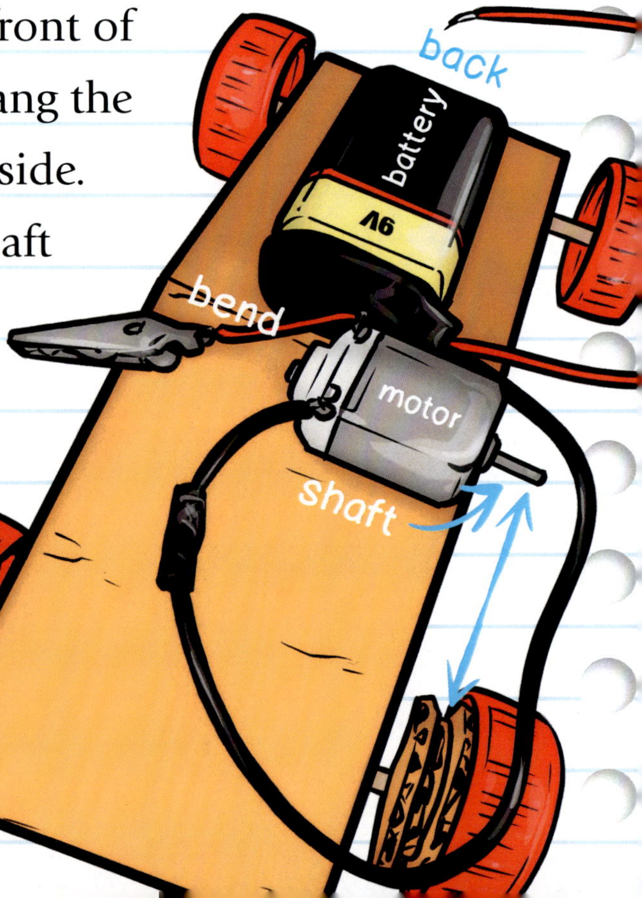

17. Clean up the wires. Fold them together, and hot glue them to the cardboard. Make sure the alligator clip reaches the exposed red wire.

18. Glue the last cardboard circle to the end of the motor's shaft.

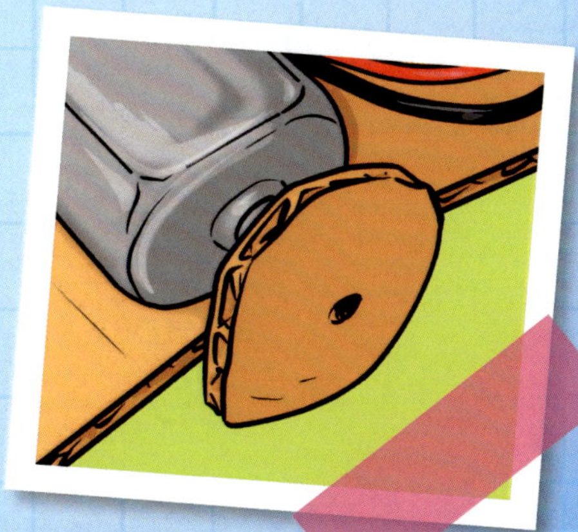

19. Put the rubber band on the motor's shaft. Then loop it over the cardboard circles on the wheel. Double up the band, if needed, so it's tight.

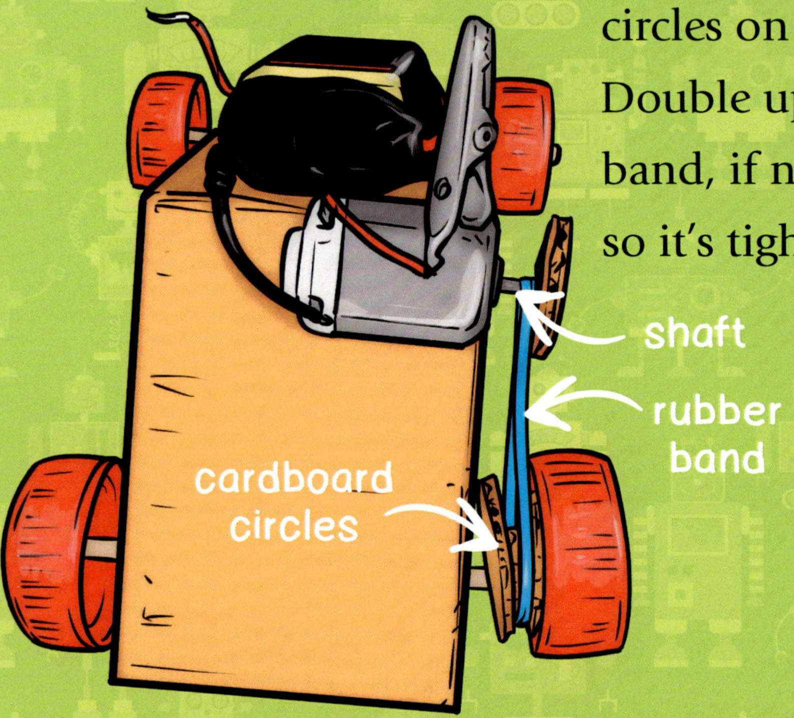

20. Measure ½ inch (1 cm) from the end of the copper wire. At that spot, bend the wire to make an "L." Then make a second "L" bend 2½ inches (6 cm) from the first.

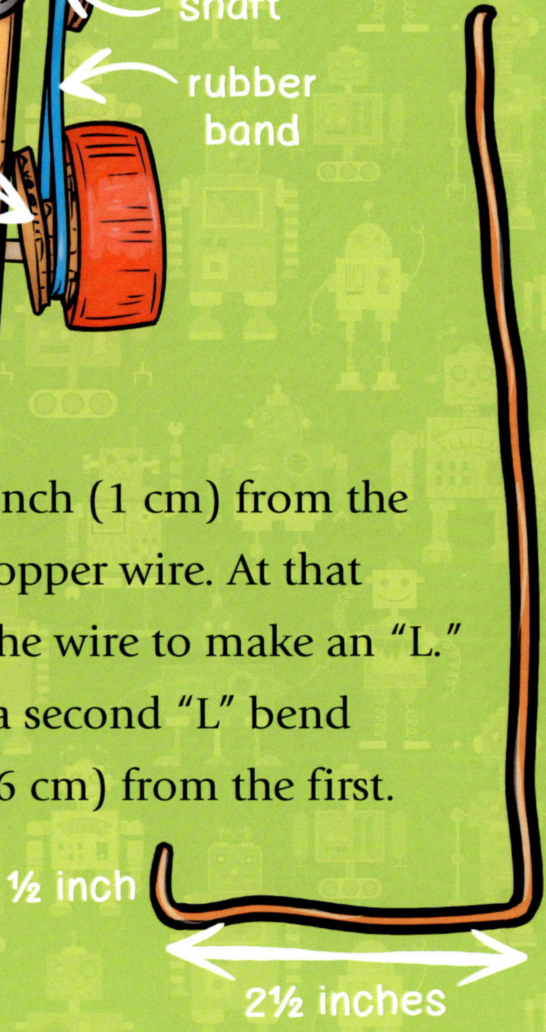

21. Thread the straight part of the wire through the middle straw. Press the short, bent part into the edge hole in the front wheel.

22. Bend the other end of the wire toward the front wheels. Make the bend about ½ inch (1 cm) from where it sticks out of the straw. Then make a little bend on the end of the wire. Stick this part in the edge hole on the wheel.

9V

23. Make your inchworm move! Clamp the alligator clip to the exposed red wire. Make sure the robot has enough space to do its crazy inching.

Chapter 3
GET IN ON THE HI JINX

Scientists use the same basic skills you did to build robots. Military robots fight in battles. Space robots explore other planets. Now you have the basic skills to make robots. How will you change the world?

Take It One Step More

1. What other materials could you use for the body?

2. What role does the rubber band play?

3. How could you build on this design? Is there a way to make this robot start and stop on its own?

GLOSSARY

clamp (KLAMP)—to hold tightly

diameter (dy-AH-muh-tur)—the length of a straight line through the center of an object

exposed (ek-SPOZD)—not covered

shaft (SHAFT)—a cylindrical bar used to support rotating pieces

uninsulated (uhn-IN-suh-lay-tuhd)—not covered with a protective coating

LEARN MORE

BOOKS

Ceceri, Kathy. *Making Simple Robots.* Sebastopol, CA: Maker Media, 2015.

Kopp, Megan. *Maker Projects for Kids Who Love Electronics.* Be a Maker! New York: Crabtree Publishing Company, 2017.

Swanson, Jennifer. *National Geographic Kids. Everything Robotics: All the Robotic Photos, Facts, and Fun!* Everything Series. Washington, D.C.: National Geographic, 2016.

WEBSITES

All about Robots
www.kidsdiscover.com/teacherresources/all-about-robots/

Build Your First Robot
www.popularmechanics.com/technology/robots/a7388/build-your-first-robot/

Robotics: Facts
idahoptv.org/sciencetrek/topics/robots/facts.cfm

TIPS AND TRICKS

Adults are boring. But they can be really helpful. Don't be afraid to ask for help if you get stuck.

If your wires don't have exposed ends, don't worry. Use a wire stripper to take off as much of the wire casing as needed. (See first tip.)

If the copper wire gets caught on the cardboard, trim off parts that are too long.

The author is super cool. He made a short video of his inchworm bot. Check it out on Black Rabbit Books' YouTube channel.